W0082840

POETRY AND THE
SCIENCE OF COMPASSION

PROFESSOR PATRICK PIETRONI

FRESCO BOOKS

CONTENTS

This volume is dedicated to Professor Paul Gilbert OBE
who has done the most to ensure the study of
compassion is underpinned by a
scientific understanding.

BODY—MIND—SPIRIT

Waking up demands so much effort

And is rewarded by the visitation of sloth
The mind not yet in charge
Allows the body to tell the tale

The breathing, shallow and rapid
The eyes, heavy with sorrow
The mouth, sticky with spittle
The limbs, ache with the burden

Slowly the mind takes over
For it is tasked so to do
The future is its journey
The body is left with the past

In those few moments between the two
Is when the spirit whispers the truth.

"Your body carries the scars
Left by your mind that has lost its way
WAKE UP! Be still, breathe slowly and listen.
Carry the past with you
For the maps are wrapped up in your skin"

Patrick Pietroni [1]

INTRODUCTION

In the first volume of this series I introduced the concept of compassion and how Charles Darwin's research suggests that the human species has evolved to behave compassionately, or at least, that we have the capacity to do so. In the *Descent of Man,* he wrote:

> *We are ... impelled to relieve the sufferings of another, in order that our own painful feelings may be at the same time relieved. In like manner we are led to participate in the pleasures of others.*[2]

Recent discoveries in neuroscience and neural-imaging support this biological basis for compassion, but it was Darwin who originally argued that,

> *"[T]hose communities which contained the greatest number of the most sympathetic members would flourish best, and rear the greatest number of offspring".*[3]

I then outlined using selected poems how the following concepts of compassion could be understood:

Proximal compassion
Distal compassion
Global compassion
Self-compassion
Compassion fatigue

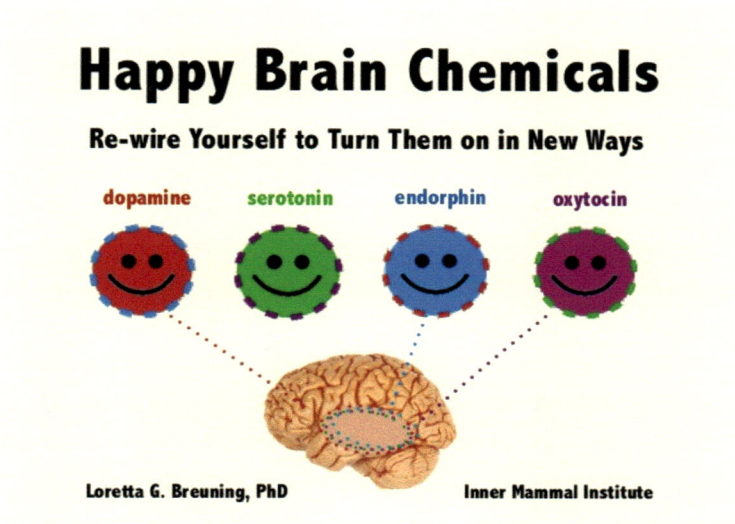

Fig. 1. Happy Brain Chemicals

Now, in this second volume, again using selected poems, I will outline how science, especially neuroscience, allows us to understand the biological, chemical and physical basis of the nature of compassion.

I will draw on Loretta Breuning's excellent slide show on *Happy Brain Chemicals*[4], and add some of the "scientific" knowledge together with a poem that addresses the effect of these chemicals on our brains. Also, the importance of the vagus nerve has recently been accepted as a major factor in how we can begin to regulate the flow of these chemicals (neuro-transmitters). I will describe the effects of oxytocin, dopamine, endomorphin, serotonin and cortisol.

First, a brief, general introduction: In the last ten years there has been a major acceleration in our understanding of brain function. Partly, this has arisen from the technology that has allowed us to see how the brain "lights up" whilst we are actively trying to solve a problem, read a poem or peacefully sleep. Neural imagining, as this is called, has allowed us to actually see how the neurons (the connecting pathways of our nervous system) actually work.

The second development references how chemical substances act as "neuromodulators". They facilitate the transfer of electrical activity between one neuron and another. It would be simplistic to say that each neurotransmitter is linked to a specific outcome, because many activate other chemicals which make causes and effects that are not as simple as we would like to believe. Think of it as one electric switch that can at the same time light up only one lamp or light up a sequence of lamps.

If this simplistic explanation of the neuroscience of compassion is not helpful, the following poem by Rajeet Singh should be. It is appropriately called *A Poem on Meaning.*

A POEM ON MEANING

Emotional is poetry
its touch reaches deep within
Strokes the fabric of being
Considers logic a sin

We humans feel by nature
To understand, we cannot begin
We think only in higher mind
While driven by urges deep within

We are products of chemical
Cortisol, Serotonin
Love exists from and in the senses
Dopamine, Oxytocin

What does it mean to be human?
Can we say? Give definition?
Or will our meaning remain always obscure
Forever pondering our creation?

Rajeet Singh [5]

Wordcloud — Science of Compassion

How does compassion fit into the science and chemistry of the neurotransmitters and autonomic nervous system? The word-cloud above only partially helps. Academics from a wide variety of disciplines, each undertaking extensive research, have ensured that the study of compassion will, if it has not already, become a contested subject. I realised this when I was giving a talk to a group of anthropologists and sociologists. It was clear after the first ten minutes that my "lecture" was not going down well. Finally, one of the more senior members of the audience stood up and exclaimed, "I am sorry, Professor Pietroni. We in this department use the term 'pro-social behaviour' as we feel compassion is too vague a term to be useful."

Newton, 1795–c.1805   William Blake

William Blake was the first poet to warn against the limitations of Newtonian Science, not only in his poetry, but also in his magnificent painting. So, I also suggest caution when linking the chemical and neurological understanding of compassion too literally.

To see compassion in your dopamine
And kindness in your oxytocin
To dominate, use only serotonin
And make sure you have endorphin before you empathise
Remember though, that none of the above will make you very wise.[6]

Or as the master put it much more elegantly in *Auguries of Innocence*:

AUGURIES OF INNOCENCE

To see a World in a Grain of Sand

And a Heaven in a Wild Flower

Hold Infinity in the palm of your hand

And Eternity in an hour

William Blake [7]

Oxytocin

Oxytocin is sometimes called the "love hormone". It is produced
in the brain and is associated with a number of specific responses.
The following list should be viewed with caution as oxytocin can
sometimes produce the opposite response to the one with which
it is more commonly associated. It is raised in "romantic attach-
ments" and high levels are present at orgasm (females). Its release
is linked to "feelings of warmth", and to one's ability to bond and
trust. However, if the pair-bonding is under threat then it would
appear that oxytocin is increased and aggressive responses are
enabled. Oxytocin is released in the final stages of giving birth
and helps to dilate the cervix. Most commonly, it facilitates the
flow of milk in the lactating mother and is released when the nipples
are stimulated. A nasal spray of oxytocin has been shown to enable
and increase the "compassionate response" to someone suffering,
especially if he or she is from the same class, ethnic, or cultural
background.

Tony Hargreaves' poem says it all:

INFANT MIND

The infant mind takes it in
mothers heartbeat
da dum da dum da dum
life rhythm set

warmth flows
flesh on flesh
lactic odour of breast

senses seed the cuddle hormone
the love creator
cosy secure all is well
oxytocin primed

feeling secure
ready to give love
receive love
the balanced child

but think of those
deprived of the hormone
who later in life

seek substitute love
solace from sad sources

Tony Hargreaves [8]

Dopamine

Dopamine is one of those chemicals that acts on many different parts of the body by sending signals to other nerve cells. It can be compared to a conductor of an orchestra who is able to control the release of different "sounds" from the different instruments in the orchestra. Dopamine's principal function is to act by producing "pleasure feelings" and is often known as the "reward/pleasure hormone". Many pleasurable experiences including sex, playing games and eating will be accompanied by dopamine release. It is also released by the use of addictive drugs (cocaine, methamphetamine) which leads to these drugs becoming addictive.

The concept of "feel-good" compassion is mitigated through the release of dopamine. Dopamine has many other functions. Its absence as a result of malfunction of the cells in the brain that manufacture it, is thought to be the main cause of Parkinson's disease.

I have chosen two poems which describe both its link to addiction as well as to the pleasure of being held and touched which may explain why touching and hugging can provide such comfort in those who are distressed.

ADDICTION

Outside,
a tendril wafts into the nose —
A pleasant olfactory response as the molecules
*   are absorbed and work into the capillaries*
Traveling through the veins,
Into the heart and then the arteries to the brain,
Binding to and activating the nicotinic receptors —
Causing a release of dopamine —
Yes, a runner's high!
And never mind the downsides,
Even after a 30 year quit.

J V Beauprex [9]

IMBALANCE

His transient touch
Taught me to love
Elusive hands embraced
Inverted beneath skin's layers,
A plastic pin point impression
That prickly sensation
Lasted for years
Hollowed hands turned every touch
Into white noise
Soft static buzzing eardrums
Burrowed deep beneath
Old memories, sneaking in
Through dopamine
Vibrating neurons numb
Until I can't sleep

Cassidy Johncox [10]

Endomorphin

Endomorphin, sometimes commonly known as endorphin, is the body's own opiate derivative, i.e. morphine, and acts to mask and relieve pain. Having a good night's sleep is increasingly linked to levels of wellbeing and the capacity to develop resilience and respond compassionately not only to oneself (self-compassion), but to the plight of others. Sleep disturbance is most commonly reported in times of stress. Endomorphins not only reduce pain but allow us to be "put to sleep" when both our body and our brain can recover their equilibrium. The side effects of our own endomorphins are much less than those produced by the addiction to morphine-like drugs. Every parent is aware of how helping an infant to go to sleep peacefully can be listed as one of the most compassionate acts they can give to their offspring.

In Shakespeare's *Hamlet's* famous soliloquy, "To be or not to be" is followed by the lines:

> *To die — to sleep, no more; and by a sleep to say we end the heart-ache and the thousand natural shocks that flesh is heir to: 'tis a consummation devoutly to be wish'd. To die, to sleep; to sleep, perchance to dream — ay, there's the rub: for in that sleep of death what dreams may come.*[11]

In his Sonnet 43, which Shakespeare wrote when he was away from his good friend, he demonstrates how dreams can have both a positive "endomorphic" effect when he dreams of his absent friend:

SONNET 43

When most I wink then do mine eyes best see,
For all the day they view things unrespected:
But when I sleep, in dreams they look on
thee,
And darkly bright are bright in dark direction;
Then thou, whose shadow shadows doth
make bright,
How would they shadow's form form happy
show
To the clear day with thy much clearer light,
When to unseeing eyes thy shade shines
so?
How would, I say, mine eyes be blessed
made
By looking on thee in the living day,
When in dead night thy fair imperfect shade
Through heavy sleep on sightless eyes doth
stay?
All days are nights to see till I see thee,
And nights bright days when dreams do
show thee me.

William Shakespeare [12]

Charlotte Smith's more recent sonnet again affirms the importance of sleep and dreams in the way our brain works to relieve stress whilst we sleep:

TO SLEEP

Come, balmy Sleep! tired Nature's soft resort!
On these sad temples all thy poppies shed;
And bid gay dreams, from Morpheus' airy court,
Float in light vision round my aching head!
Secure of all thy blessings, partial Power!
On his hard bed the peasant throws him down;
And the poor sea-boy, in the rudest hour,
Enjoys thee more than he who wears a crown.
Clasp'd in her faithful shepherd's guardian arms,
Well may the village-girl sweet slumbers prove;
And they, O gentle Sleep! still taste thy charms,
Who wake to labour, liberty, and love.
But still thy opiate aid dost thou deny
To calm the anxious breast, to close the streaming eye.

Charlotte Smith [13]

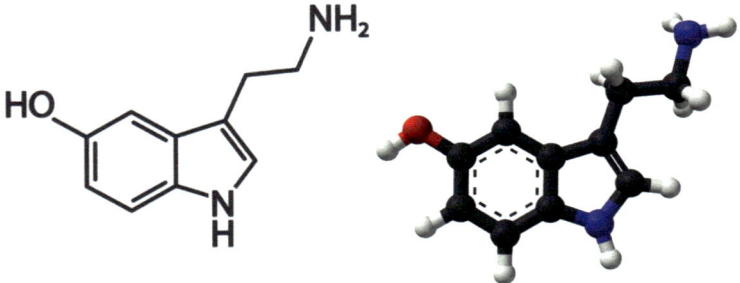

Serotonin

Serotonin has many different functions in both humans and animals. It can act on its own or as a neurotransmitter stimulating the release of other hormones, including dopamine. It is related to the regulation of mood, appetite, sleep, memory, learning and blood clotting! It is either not sufficiently released, or if too much of it is present it effects the bowels (constipation, irritable bowels and sexual behavior). In relation to social behavior and compassion, it stimulates pro-social behavior (the empathic response to the needs of another) and in males is associated with social dominance and "feeling good about one's self". Laughter is linked to serotonin release as is the "calm sense" of knowing you have won.

Serotonin is a toxic substance and is not available as a medicine (see poems). It is the substance that causes pain if you are stung by a hornet or wasp. Serotonin is found in chocolate and often induces or produces the romantic experience of love and stimulating sexual desire.

The following poems are chosen to illustrate its many physiological effects.

SEROTONIN

Dear Serotonin,
It's been many years since I've seen you last
Since you up and left me in the past
From then I've never been the same
And your absence from me is my shame

When you first left, I was a wreck
Life was a thorn in my side and a pain in my neck
On the verge of destruction and utter collapse
On a broken record of constant relapse

I didn't give up, and I sought help
Heading to recovery; a push, a pull, a skelp
I fought through and I was strong
And I'm still fighting this and pushing it along

I'm going through my days without drugs or medication
Getting by day-by-day holding onto motivation
All those drugs would make you come back worse
I am beating what you've done to me; undoing this whole curse

I could blame you, blame myself, or could just blame genetics
But making up any excuse just makes me look pathetic
I accept who I am and where I'm at in life
I will continue to fight you; nail and tooth and knife

No matter what you do to me, I will never go away
I can feel myself getting stronger with every passing day
You have finally met your match, the battle has begun
I will end this everlasting war, in my name it shall be won

Yours Truly, Dylan Foss [14]

CHOCOLATE MOUSSE CAKE

I can die happy, with a great big grin
Knowing that I'm going to submit to this sin
It's salacious, it's scandalous — I'm in a tailspin
Chocolate Mousse Cake Give it up, give in — Dig in!

Each delectable forkful
An endorphin rush
Serotonin gush
My heart races, my cheeks flush
A decadent delectation
A sweeter than sweet sensation
I succumb to the temptation

A morsel of mousse
So silky, so dreamy
Rich, moist cake
So milky, so creamy
Dark and mysterious
I'm giddy — delirious
My oh so perfect lover
This relationship is serious

I fall into your sensual embrace
And lick the plate clean, there is no trace
My mantra is "Mmmmmm" So I freely partake
Never get enough
Of this divine stuff
My slice of heaven
Chocolate Mousse Cake

Corinne Curcio [15]

IMPENDING SENSE OF NAP

Brain is crackling, crisp, ivory bone dry
Gremlin stuffing cotton behind my eyes

Head begins to swell with torpidity
Vivid mind fading to transparency

Internal membranes breaking down
Thoughts run a deep molasses brown

'Tween thought and motion, expanding rift
Act of sheer will, the body to lift

Limbs grow wooden, ready to fall
Seek out the blessed horizontal

Cover exhaustion with soft frayed quilt
Self-indulgent moment's guilt

Serotonin sleep dump almost disappointing
Blessed moment of irresponsibility ending

Leaden lids descend on eyes
Fading into a sky blue paradise

Tom Quigley [16]

Cortisol

Cortisol, often known as the "stress hormone", is produced by the adrenal glands situated on top of the kidneys. It is released into the blood stream and stimulated by a substance ACTH, which is produced by the pituitary gland in the brain.

Cortisol levels are increased by stress as well as when the level of blood sugar is decreased. It suppresses the immune system response to allergies and insect bites. It has a 24-hour diurnal level, which is lowest during sleep and peaks a few hours after waking.

Its effect on one's capacity to be empathetic to others' distress and to act compassionately is now much better understood. We are all (probably!) familiar with the occasions when under stress, i.e. raised cortisol, we are less likely to respond to other people's distress. A raised cortisol level, it would seem, inhibits our capacity to respond compassionately. However, it would appear that the opposite may also be true. If you are unable to respond to stressful situations yourself by releasing cortisol, you are more likely to exhibit indifference or "cross the street" when you witness someone else's distress. People with lower levels of cortisol are less able to respond empathetically or with compassion and are often described as "cold" or "careless". In contrast, those of us who respond to stress well and have learnt how to adapt to the challenges we meet, including the loss of a loved one, manifest the ability to respond to others' distress. Those of us who have close loving relationships are more likely to respond with empathy and concern. Compassion to others often enables us to manage our own stress more effectively. It is the sustained level of cortisol that is a result of repeated and frequent stress events that leads to physical and psychological disorders (depression, anxiety, poor sleep, raised blood pressure, post traumatic stress, etc.).

So, the message the scientists wish to make is:

Learn to understand the factors that reduce cortisol levels:
a.   Omega 3 fatty acids (fish oils)
b.   Exercise (walking, dancing)
c.   Touch/massage/hugs
d.   Laughter
e.   Listening to music
f.   Good night's sleep

Factors that increase cortisol levels:

a.   Trauma and stressful events (divorce, unemployment, death of a loved one)
b.   Problematic alcohol
c.   Sleep deprivation
d.   Addiction to drugs

UNTOLD FEELING

The happiness I get after writing
Something soothing my soul, be like
Cortisol released after drinking
Hot coffee in winter evening.

Anila Ankireddi [17]

CORTISOL POOLS

The shivers in the night, the quiet inner fight
really, victory for me is a night of rest
I often cool my hot body, shield it from peace
divingboard summersaults into a pool of cortisol
dissolved alkaseltzers of pending doom
and black roses sprinkled on top for effect
pool of cortisol, you can have it all
telling me it's ok, won't make it go away
telling me to rest, brain refuses to compromise
so it whips the heart to race faster
she said she couldn't find me
look for the scotch trails, heart bits, and cigarette
smoke signals, awaiting there by the
light blue cortisol pool, baby,
sincerely peace I sit here waiting for you.

Julien Grey [18]

THE HOUSE OF CORTISOL

My blood runs by touch
Through the valleys of my body's darkness
My heart is cartilage hutch
Steadily rips through the silence.

The seahorses of hormones
Are wild and messing my endocrine ocean
I feel it in my bones
With my unstable emotions.

The house of Cortisol rises
On a peak of imminent death.
I hope the life will surprise me
And switch egress with ingress.

Life asks for a bit of devotion
Life is the major cause of mortality rate.
It hands out a sinister potion
And tells you to drink up and wait.

Anna L Shtorm [19]

Vagus Nerve

Vagus nerve activity is of particular importance to emotional regulation. Compassion is linked to the activity in the autonomic nervous system — primarily the vagus nerve.

Vagus is the tenth cranial nerve originating in the stem of the brain and is the longest nerve in the body. It innervates the lungs, heart, stomach, liver, spleen, pancreas, right kidney and the small and large intestines. The vagus is the part of the parasympathetic nervous system responsible for regulating heart rate and respiratory rate. It can be considered to balance out the sympathetic nervous system, which activates the fight/flight response to stress and can help return the stress response to a more neutral state, i.e. slow the heart rate and reduce the respiratory rate of breathing. The fact that we can have conscious control over what is known as the vagal-tone gives us the option of activating the parasympathetic system and modulate the bodies response to stressful events. Think of the vagus as the brake in a runaway car. Sympathetic discharge is the accelerator and parasympathetic response is the brake pedal.

There is no doubt in my mind that probably the most important self-help exercise we can engage in is to learn how to use our breathing to help modulate and balance our respiratory rate. Understanding the way in which we breathe can allow us to manage stressful states and stimulate those five hormones that we now know are involved in the emergence of empathic, prosocial and compassionate responses to the challenges we will inevitably meet in our lifetime.

The ancient Yogis in their caves many centuries ago discovered through practice the method they labeled "pranayama". As a medical student and young doctor I had no such teaching, but after some years studying with my Guru and using the Western scientific method to measure and monitor this ancient wisdom, I concur with the ancient philosophers who used to say the body was like "the Temple of God". It was necessary to keep the temple clean, peaceful and well-attended so that one might hear the voice of God more clearly. We do not need to accept this exact comparison to appreciate that our bodies need to be looked after if our minds and spirit are to function well.

There has been progress in Western practice, where mindfulness, meditation and relaxation classes are much more available and no longer considered cranky.

I will end this booklet with a longish section on breathing and the breath. This does not require you to know about the five "happiness chemicals" as Loretta Breuning called them, but knowing about both the "happiness chemicals' and the importance of the breath will allow you to develop self-compassion as well as your capacity to act compassionately to those less fortunate than yourself.

BREATHING

Even though breathing is the most important and vital act we do, we rarely give much thought to how we breathe. If we stop breathing, we die. We recognize this fact in our language when we talk about someone "expiring" and conversely, we talk about being "inspired" and taking a "good breath in" as ways of achieving positive health. Most of us recognize that our breathing alters in pattern and rhythm throughout the day. How that breathing alters may be influenced by how we feel. Again, we talk about "gasping for breath" or "catching one's breath" or we say that something "took my breath away". We may also be aware of how our breathing increases when we get excited or how we sigh when we are sad or depressed. On occasions we may stop breathing altogether for as much as half a minute, and it is not uncommon for some children to have breath-holding attacks which are often associated with anger and temper tantrums.

One of the most important facts about breathing is that it can take place without our thinking about it and also that we can alter it at will. We can slow down or increase our breathing if we choose to. It is one of the very few activities of the body in which there is both conscious control and automative activity. This breathing forms a link between the conscious and unconscious parts of our being. By observing and increasing the awareness of our breathing, we can obtain useful information as to how our whole being is operating. Breathing is the most sensitive indicator or warning sign that we possess. Consciously increasing one's awareness about breathing and practicing some of the breathing exercises I will describe can be the most important steps anyone can take to improve their wellbeing, decrease the level of stress and help to bring about a sense of the interconnections between body, mind and spirit.

How do we breathe?

Breathing is the activity that brings oxygen from the atmosphere into the lungs and expels carbon dioxide and other waste products from the lungs into the atmosphere. The lungs are situated in the chest, covered by a thin but tough layer called the pleura, and surrounded by the ribs and muscles of respiration. The muscles of respiration are of three types:

1. (Inter)-Costal muscles
   Muscles between the ribs on the chest wall.
2. Diaphragm
   Dome-shaped muscles separating the chest cavity from the abdominal contents.
3. Accessory muscles of respiration
   These are situated at the top end of the rib cage together with some muscles of the back and abdomen.

Chest breathing

This is characterized by an upward and outward movement of the chest due to contraction of the costal (rib) muscles. This type of breathing is found most typically during vigorous exercise or in emergency situations. It allows the chest to expand quickly and is the most efficient way of obtaining oxygen quickly. Chest breathing may also help to arouse us and you may find yourself taking a deep breath and expanding your chest when you first wake up. Using the costal muscle for breathing, however, is not the "normal" or "natural" way for us to breathe during other situations not associated with exercise or arousal. Even so, what happens for many individuals is that they maintain a costal pattern of breathing even following the cessation of the emergency situation. A constant use of chest breathing keeps the body in a state of constant arousal and the body acts as if it is experiencing a stressor. Let me give you an illustration.

Imagine you are driving a car and suddenly a small child runs across the road. Your immediate reaction is to slam on the brakes, grip the steering wheel, tighten your muscles, breathe more rapidly with an exaggerated inspiration or gasp. You just miss the child and start accelerating again. You may breathe a sigh of relief — breathing out forcefully — and relax your grip on the steering wheel. What may happen, however, and what often does happen, is that you maintain your high state of arousal; you still continue to breathe shallowly with your chest muscles and you still maintain your increased muscle tension. In other words, you maintain your stress response for much longer than is appropriate. Your body has now returned to a state of balance and you will have to respond to your next stressor from a position of heightened state of arousal. Learning to let go and release the tension accumulated as a result of your stress response is essential if you are to avoid the stress state.

The clue as to how to do this was given in the example and can be better understood after I can describe the second way in which we breathe.

Diaphragmatic breathing

The diaphragm is a horizontal dome-shaped muscle which separates the contents of your chest (heart and lungs) from your abdomen (stomach, liver, intestines). On inspiration, the diaphragm contracts, flattens and descends, thus creating a vacuum in the chest, and air is sucked in. As the diaphragm descends, it pushes the abdominal contents down and the increase in pressure forces the abdominal wall (the front of your abdomen) out. On expiration, the diaphragm relaxes and forces air out of the lungs, reducing the pressure on the abdominal contents and causing the abdominal wall to flatten.

It is important to note that the abdominal muscles do not normally contract during diaphragmatic breathing — they only respond passively to the increase in pressure in the abdomen. If you watch a small baby breathing you will see its abdomen moving up and down. The baby is breathing with its diaphragm, which is the normal and healthy way to breathe. When the baby cries or is hungry or distressed, the pattern of its breathing will change to a chest or costal rhythm. Unfortunately, this pattern of breathing is encouraged by such statements as "stick your chest out when you breathe" or "flatten your stomach". Thus, we develop a chronic pattern of rapid shallow chest breathing during childhood, and in adulthood consider this pattern to be normal. It may be "normal" but it is certainly unhealthy.

Diaphragmatic breathing requires less "energy" than chest breathing; it allows for expansion of the base of the lungs and the up-and-down motion of the diaphragm gently massages the abdominal organs. Chronic chest breathers breathe 12–16 full breaths a minute, whereas regular diaphragmatic breathing requires only 8-10 breaths a minute. This works out at

16,000–18,000 breaths a day in chest breathing as opposed to 8,000–11,000 in diaphragmatic breathing. Over a lifetime of breathing this can amount to a large difference in energy expanded. However, probably the most important difference as has been mentioned already, is that chronic chest breathing keeps the body and mind in a chronic state of arousal.

Mouth/nose breathing

Most of us naturally breathe through our nostrils. We are all aware of this when we are forced to breathe through our mouths when we have a cold or an allergy. Nasal breathing is important in the breathing cycle. The air is warmed and moistened in the nose before entering the lungs, but more importantly, the air stimulates delicate nerve endings in the lining of the nose which serve to reduce the level of arousal present in the body and so helps to calm the mind. Snoring and breath apnea (periods of breath holding) are associated with chronic mouth breathing and may lead to disturbances in the sensitive auto-nervous system.

Inhalation/exhalation

The breath cycle consists of inhalation and exhalation. When we were children, no one told us whether or not we should pause between breaths. Breathing retraining programmes are being introduced in several medical centres dealing with coronary disease, high blood pressure and chronic lung conditions. The "hyperventilation syndrome" (breathing pattern of rapid shallow chest breathing) accounts for many strange presentations to doctors — dizziness, chest pains, common migraine, cramps, "nervousness", phobias, etc. What we do know is that retraining individuals to breathe through their nostrils with their diaphragm in regular rhythmical patterns — where the inhallation is as long as the exhalation with little or no pause between — can produce immediate benefits that result from reducing the harmful effects of a chronic state of arousal.

Mastering the art of breathing will allow you to train as a conductor of the "happy chemicals" that are in our orchestra.

So, I end with a poem by Marilyn Lott which brings together poetry, the breath and the sound of silence.

I BREATHE POETRY

Whenever I get on the road and travel
I don't plan to write any poetry
I'll take a break, I tell myself
My vacation will be spent differently.

But everything brings on a poem
During daytime or in my dreams
I live and I breathe poetry
I just can't escape it, it seems.

So I guess I must accept who I am
And the person I have to be
For it doesn't matter my schedule
I simply breathe poetry.

Marilyn Lott [20]

References

1. Pietroni, P. (2014). *Body-Mind-Spirit*.
2. Darwin, C. (1871). *The Decent of Man,* and *Selection in Relation to Sex.* London. John Murray.
3. Darwin, C. (2004. First published 1859). *On the Origin of Species by Means of Natural Selection,* or *The Perseveration of Favoured Races in the Struggle for Life.* London. Castle Books.
4. Bruening, L. Available at https://innermammalinstitute.org/ (last accessed 11 February 2020).
5. Singh, R. (2018). *A Poem on Meaning.* Available at https://medium.com/@rajeetsingh/a-poem-on-meaning-1fb5794043bd (last accessed December 2019).
6. Pietroni, P. (2019).
7. Blake, W. (1863). *Auguries of Innocence.* Available at https://poetry foundation.org/poems/43650/auguries-of-innocence (last accessed February 2020).
8. Hargreaves, T. (2019). *Infant Mind.* Available at https://poetrysoup.com/ poem/infant_mind_1200289 (last accessed February 2020).
9. Beaupre, J.V. (2019). *Addiction.* Available at https://hellopoetry.com/ jvbeaupre/ (last accessed February 2020).
10. Johncox, C. (2018). *Imbalance.* Available at https://hellopoetry.com/ poem/2778845/imbalance/ (last accessed October 2019).
11. Shakespeare, W. (1599-1601). *The Tragedy of Hamlet, Prince of Denmark (Hamlet), Act III, Scene I [To be, or not to be].*
12. Shakespeare, W. (1609). *Sonnet 43.*
13. Smith, C. *To Sleep.* Available at https://www.poetrynook.com/ poem/sleep-92 (last accessed December 2019).
14. Foss, D. Serotonin. (2016). Available at https://poetrysoup.com/ poem/serotonin_758142 (last accessed December 2019).

15. Curcio, C. (2010). *Chocolate Mousse Cake.* Available at https://poetrysoup.com/poem/chocolate_mousse_cake_230184 (last accessed December 2019).

16. Quigley, T. (2016). *Impending Sense of Nap.* Available at https://poetrysoup.com/poem/impending_sense_of_nap_771805 (last accessed December 2019).

17. Ankireddi, A. (2019). Available at https://www.yourquote.in/anila-ankireddi-52nd/quotes/happiness-i-get-after-writing-something-soothing-my-soul-hot-m6vb2 (last accessed February 2020).

18. Grey, J. (2015). *Cortisol Pools.* https://www.powerpoetry.org/poems/cortisol-pools (last accessed February 2020).

19. Shtorm, A.L. (2019). *The House of Cortisol.* Available at https://medium.com/literally-literary/the-house-of-cortisol-11a5bc04be73(last accessed December 2019).

20. Lott, M. (2013). *I Breathe Poetry.* Available at https://www.poemhunter.com/poem/i-breathe-poetry-2 (last accessed December 2019).

Photo Credits

Loretta Breuning — Happy Brain Chemicals, p.7
Wordcloud — The Science of Compassion, p.10
Newton, 1795–c.1805   William Blake, p.11
Photo by Blair Fraser, p.31

Professor Patrick Pietroni

Professor Patrick Pietroni DSC (Hon), FRCP, FRCGP, MFPH, retired from his post as Dean of General Practice at the London University in 2001 following the re-organisation of the London Deanery.

Professor Pietroni has published several books and numerous academic articles. He founded and was editor of the *Journal of Inter-professional Care*, the *International Journal of Cuban Studies,* and the *Journal of Psychological Therapies in Primary Care.*

In 2013, Professor Pietroni organised a conference in Shrewsbury entitled "Mental Health—How could we do better?" Following this conference he established a steering group of interested senior academics to explore the concept of "compassion", its rigour and relevance in our societies. This led to a launching conference and the establishment of the Darwin Centre Trust (DCT) and the Darwin International Institute for the Study of Compassion (DIISC) in 2015. DIISC was established in December 2015 to act as the operational wing of the newly formed DCT. Spearheaded by Professor Pietroni, the DCT and DIISC are supported and guided by an international group of eminent academics, writers, and thinkers. He is currently the Director of the Centre for the Study of Compassion at University of New Mexico.

Professor Pietroni lives in Shrewsbury, Shropshire, U.K., which is the birth place of Charles Darwin. Professor Pietroni presented his choice of poems at the Annual Darwin Festival in 2019.

Publisher
SF Design, llc / Fresco Books
Albuquerque, New Mexico
frescobooks.com

ISBN: 978-1-934491-75-1

Copyright © 2020 Patrick Pietroni

Every reasonable effort has been made to acknowledge all copyright
holders. Any errors or omissions that may have occurred are inadvertent,
and anyone with any copyright queries is invited to write to the publisher,
so that a full acknowledgment may be included in subsequent editions
of this work.

All rights reserved. No part of this publication may be reproduced,
stored in a retrieval system, or transmitted, in any form or by any
means, electronic, mechanical, photocopying, recording or otherwise—
except as permitted under the United States Copyright Act—without
the prior permission of Patrick Pietroni. Nor may the pages be applied
to any materials, cut, trimmed, or sized to alter the existing trim sizes,
matted, or framed with the intent to create other products for sale or
resale or profit in any manner whatsoever, without prior permission
in writing from Patrick Pietroni.